# Twelve MONTHS Make a Year

*Written by*
*Alicia Rodriguez*

*Illustrated by*
*Alisha Monnin*

A Sunshine Picture Book

CRABTREE
Publishing Company
www.crabtreebooks.com

Twelve months make a year!

That's January, February, March, April, May, June, July, August, September, October, November, and December.

But what is a month?

A month is a unit of time, used in calendars. Some months are thirty days while others have thirty-one. And one month has only twenty-eight days. Though sometimes . . . twenty-nine!

Some months fall in winter, while others are in the spring, summer, or fall.

There are fun facts you can learn about all twelve months. Special holidays are celebrated each month. There's even a birthstone (a pretty colored gemstone) and flower for each month.

Ready to learn about the months? Just turn the page to find out some of the things that make the twelve months of the year special.

**January** is the first month of the year and a time for new beginnings.

On January 1, we celebrate New Year's Day. It's the perfect time to look back on everything you did in the past year and decide what things you want to try in the coming year.

In the Northern Hemisphere, January falls in the winter. But in the Southern Hemisphere, the seasons are reversed, and January is in the summer.

Sound confusing? It's really not! Think of an imaginary line that runs around the middle of planet Earth. It's called the equator. All of the countries north of the equator are in the Northern Hemisphere. And all of the countries to the south of it are in the Southern Hemisphere.

January was named for the Roman god, Janus. He has two faces, one that looks forward and one that looks backward. Janus makes us think about beginnings and endings.

There are 31 days in January.

The birthstone of January is a garnet. The flowers of January are a carnation and a snowdrop.

**February** is the second month of the year. It's also the shortest month.

February has 28 days. But almost every fourth year, an extra day is added to the calendar year and that day falls in February. When a 29th day is added to February, it is called a leap day.

In the Northern Hemisphere, the weather is cold in February. Some places even get snow! February is a great month to bundle up and enjoy the winter weather.

A fun fact about February: it is the most misspelled month of the year.

# BLACK HISTORY MONTH

February is named after an ancient Roman festival called Februa, which was used to prepare for the coming of spring.

Lots of holidays are celebrated in February, such as Valentine's Day, President's Day, and Chinese New Year.

Black History Month is also observed in February.

The February birthstone is an amethyst. The flowers of February are a violet and a primrose.

**March** is the third month of the year and has 31 days.

In the Northern Hemisphere, March is the end of winter and the beginning of spring. Leaves open, flowers blossom, and animals start to come out of hibernation.

But in the Southern Hemisphere, the seasons are the opposite. March is the beginning of fall!

The name March comes from Mars, the Roman god of war. In ancient times, troops would wait for winter to end before they would go off to battle.

St. Patrick's Day, an Irish holiday, is celebrated in March.

Sometimes, the Christian holiday, Easter, falls in March and so does Passover, a Jewish holiday. Other years these holidays fall a little later and are in April.

International Women's Day is also celebrated in March.

The birthstone of March is an aquamarine or a bloodstone. The flower is a daffodil.

**April** is the fourth month of the year and has 30 days.

In many places, it rains a lot during the month of April, which helps flowers grow. Lots of rain also means lots of fun. Look for a puddle and start jumping!

No one is sure where April got its name. But we do know that the word "April" comes from the Latin verb "aperire," which means "to open." Maybe it's because all of the flowers are opening!

There are lots of holiday celebrations in April.

The first day of April is called April Fool's Day. This holiday is about playing tricks and practical jokes.

Earth Day is also celebrated in April. On April 22nd of each year, over a billion people around the world do something on this day to help the environment.

The April birthstone is a diamond. The flowers of April are a daisy and a sweet pea.

**May** is the fifth month of the year and has 31 days.

It is known as a month of transition. In the Northern Hemisphere, flowers are blooming, birds are chirping, and summer is on the way.

May is named for Maia, the Greek goddess who looked after plants.

Mother's Day is in May. So is Teacher Appreciation Week and Memorial Day, when the United States honors members of the military who died serving their country.

Fun Fact about May: In May of 1931, the Empire State Building opened in New York City. At the time, it was the tallest building in the world.

The May birthstone is an emerald. The flowers of May are a lily of the valley and a hawthorne.